THE BUCK IN THE SNOW
AND OTHER POEMS

The

BUCK IN THE SNOW

& Other Poems by

EDNA ST. VINCENT MILLAY

HARPER & BROTHERS *Publishers*

New York *and* London

MCMXXVIII

CONTENTS

Part One

Part Two

Part Three

PART FOUR

PART ONE

MORITURUS

If I could have
  Two things in one:
The peace of the grave,
  And the light of the sun;

My hands across
  My thin breast-bone,
But aware of the moss
  Invading the stone,

Aware of the flight
  Of the golden flicker
With his wing to the light;
  To hear him nicker

And drum with his bill
  On the rotted willow;
Snug and still
  On a grey pillow

Deep in the clay
  Where digging is hard,
Out of the way,—
  The blue shard

Of a broken platter—
    If I might be
Insensate matter
    With sensate me

Sitting within,
    Harking and prying,
I might begin
    To dicker with dying.

For the body at best
    Is a bundle of aches,
Longing for rest;
    It cries when it wakes

"Alas, 'tis light!"
    At set of sun
"Alas, 'tis night,
    And nothing done!"

Death, however,
    Is a spongy wall,
Is a sticky river,
    Is nothing at all.

Summon the weeper,
   Wail and sing;
Call him Reaper,
   Angel, King;

Call him Evil
   Drunk to the lees,
Monster, Devil,—
   He is less than these.

Call him Thief,
   The Maggot in the Cheese,
The Canker in the Leaf,—
   He is less than these.

Dusk without sound,
   Where the spirit by pain
Uncoiled, is wound
   To spring again;

The mind enmeshed
   Laid straight in repose,
And the body refreshed
   By feeding the rose,—

These are but visions;
   These would be

The grave's derisions,
    Could the grave see.

Here is the wish
    Of one that died
Like a beached fish
    On the ebb of the tide:

That he might wait
    Till the tide came back,
To see if a crate,
    Or a bottle, or a black

Boot, or an oar,
    Or an orange peel
Be washed ashore. . . .
    About his heel

The sand slips;
    The last he hears
From the world's lips
    Is the sand in his ears.

What thing is little?—
    The aphis hid
In a house of spittle?
    The hinge of the lid

Of the spider's eye
  At the spider's birth?
"Greater am I
  By the earth's girth

"Than Mighty Death!"
  All creatures cry
That can summon breath;—
  And speak no lie.

For He is nothing;
  He is less
Than Echo answering
  "Nothingness!"—

Less than the heat
  Of the furthest star
To the ripening wheat;
  Less by far,

When all the lipping
  Is said and sung,
Than the sweat dripping
  From a dog's tongue.

This being so,
  And I being such,

I would liever go
    On a cripple's crutch,

Lopped and felled;
    Liever be dependent
On a chair propelled
    By a surly attendant

With a foul breath,
    And be spooned my food,
Than go with Death
    Where nothing good,

Not even the thrust
    Of the summer gnat,
Consoles the dust
    For being that.

Needy, lonely,
    Stitched by pain,
Left with only
    The drip of the rain

Out of all I had;
    The books of the wise,
Badly read
    By other eyes,

Lewdly bawled
    At my closing ear;
Hated, called
    A lingerer here;—

Withstanding Death
    Till Life be gone,
I shall treasure my breath,
    I shall linger on.

I shall bolt my door
    With a bolt and a cable;
I shall block my door
    With a bureau and a table;

With all my might
    My door shall be barred.
I shall put up a fight,
    I shall take it hard.

With his hand on my mouth
    He shall drag me forth,
Shrieking to the south
    And clutching at the north.

SONG

Gone, gone again is Summer the lovely.
  She that knew not where to hide,
Is gone again like a jeweled fish from the hand,
  Is lost on every side.

Mute, mute, I make my way to the garden,
  Thither where she last was seen;
The heavy foot of the frost is on the flags there,
  Where her light step has been.

Gone, gone again is Summer the lovely,
  Gone again on every side,
Lost again like a shining fish from the hand
  Into the shadowy tide.

TO THE WIFE OF A SICK FRIEND

SHELTER this candle from the wind.
Hold it steady. In its light
The cave wherein we wander lost
Glitters with frosty stalactite,
Blossoms with mineral rose and lotus,
Sparkles with crystal moon and star,
Till a man would rather be lost than found:
We have forgotten where we are.

Shelter this candle. Shrewdly blowing
Down the cave from a secret door
Enters our only foe, the wind.
Hold it steady. Lest we stand,
Each in a sudden, separate dark,
The hot wax spattered upon your hand,
The smoking wick in my nostrils strong,
The inner eyelid red and green
For a moment yet with moons and roses,—
Then the unmitigated dark.

Alone, alone, in a terrible place,
In utter dark without a face,
With only the dripping of the water on the stone,
And the sound of your tears, and the taste of my
    own.

THE BOBOLINK

Black bird scudding
Under the rainy sky,
How wet your wings must be!
And your small head how sleek and cold with
     water.

Oh, Bobolink, 'tis you!
Over the buffeted orchard in the summer draught,
Chuckling and singing, charging the rainy cloud,
A little bird gone daft,
A little bird with a secret.

Only the bobolink on the rainy
Rhubarb blossom,
Knows my heart.
For whom adversity has not a word to say that
     can be heard
Above the din of summer.
The rain has taught us nothing. And the hooves of
     cattle, and the cat in the grass
Have taught us nothing.
The hawk that motionless above the hill
In the pure sky
Stands like a blackened planet
Has taught us nothing,—seeing him shut his wings
     and fall

Has taught us nothing at all.
In the shadow of the hawk we feather our nests.

Bobolink, you and I, an airy fool and an earthy,
Chuckling under the rain!

I shall never be sad again.
I shall never be sad again.

Ah, sweet, absurd,
Belovèd, bedraggled bird!

THE HAWKWEED

BETWEEN the red-top and the rye,
　　Between the buckwheat and the corn,
The ploughman sees with sullen eye
The hawkweed licking at the sky:

　　Three level acres all forlorn,
　　Unfertile, sour, outrun, outworn,
　　Free as the day that they were born.

Southward and northward, west and east,
　　The sulphate and the lime are spread;
Harrowed and sweetened, urged, increased,
The furrow sprouts for man and beast:

　　While of the hawkweed's radiant head
　　No stanchion reeks, no stock is fed.

Triumphant up the taken field
　　The tractor and the plough advance;
Blest be the healthy germ concealed
In the rich earth, and blest the yield:

　　And blest be Beauty, that enchants
　　The frail, the solitary lance.

TO A FRIEND ESTRANGED FROM ME

Now goes under, and I watch it go under, the sun
That will not rise again.
Today has seen the setting, in your eyes cold and
      senseless as the sea,
Of friendship better than bread, and of bright
      charity
That lifts a man a little above the beasts that run.

That this could be!
That I should live to see
Most vulgar Pride, that stale obstreperous clown,
So fitted out with purple robe and crown
To stand among his betters! Face to face
With outraged me in this once holy place,
Where Wisdom was a favoured guest and hunted
      Truth was harboured out of danger,
He bulks enthroned, a lewd, an insupportable
      stranger!

I would have sworn, indeed I swore it:
The hills may shift, the waters may decline,
Winter may twist the stem from the twig that
      bore it,
But never your love from me, your hand from
      mine.

Now goes under the sun, and I watch it go under.
Farewell, sweet light, great wonder!
You, too, farewell,—but fare not well enough to
    dream
You have done wisely to invite the night before
    the darkness came.

THE ROAD TO AVRILLÉ

APRIL again in Avrillé,
  And the brown lark in air.
And you and I a world apart,
  That walked together there.

The cuckoo spoke from out the wood,
  The lark from out the sky.
Embraced upon the highway stood
  Love-sick you and I.

The rosy peasant left his bees,
  The carrier slowed his cart,
To shout us blithe obscenities,
  And bless us from the heart,

That long before the year was out,
  Under the autumn rain,
Far from the road to Avrillé,
  Parted with little pain.

FOR PAO-CHIN,
A BOATMAN ON THE YELLOW SEA

Where is he now, in his soiled shirt reeking of
    garlic,
Sculling his sampan home, and night approaching
    fast—
The red sail hanging wrinkled on the bamboo mast;

Where is he now, I shall remember my whole life
    long
With love and praise, for the sake of a small song
Played on a Chinese flute?
                 I have been sad;
I have been in cities where the song was all I had,—
A treasure never to be bartered by the hungry days.

Where is he now, for whom I carry in my heart
This love, this praise?

NORTHERN APRIL

O MIND, beset by music never for a moment quiet,—
The wind at the flue, the wind strumming the
    shutter;
The soft, antiphonal speech of the doubled brook,
    never for a moment quiet;
The rush of the rain against the glass, his voice in
    the eaves-gutter!

Where shall I lay you to sleep, and the robins be
    quiet?
Lay you to sleep—and the frogs be silent in the
    marsh?
Crashes the sleet from the bough and the bough
    sighs upward, never for a moment quiet.
April is upon us, pitiless and young and harsh.

O April, full of blood, full of breath, have pity upon
    us!
Pale, where the winter like a stone has been lifted
    away, we emerge like yellow grass.
Be for a moment quiet, buffet us not, have pity
    upon us,
Till the green come back into the vein, till the
    giddiness pass.

THERE AT DUSK I FOUND YOU

THERE at dusk I found you, walking and weeping
Upon the broken flags,
Where at dusk the dumb white nicotine awakes and
    utters her fragrance
In a garden sleeping.

Looking askance you said:
Love is dead.

Under our eyes without warning softly the summer
    afternoon let fall
The rose upon the wall,
And it lay there spintered.
Terribly then into my heart the forgotten anguish
    entered.

I saw the dark stone on the smallest finger of
    your hand,
And the clean cuff above.
No more, no more the dark stone on the smallest
    finger
Of your brown and naked arm,
Lifting my body in love!

Worse than dead is he of the wounded wing,
Who walks between us, weeping upon the cold
　　flags,
Bleeding and weeping, dragging his broken wing.
He has gathered the rose into his hand and chafed
　　her with his breath.
But the rose is quiet and pale. She has forgotten
　　us all.
Even spring.
Even death.

As for me, I have forgotten nothing,—nor shall I
　　ever forget—
But this one thing:
I have forgotten which of us it was
That hurt his wing.
I only know his limping flight above us in the blue
　　air
Toward the sunset cloud
Is more than I can bear.

You, you there,
Stiff-necked and angry, holding up your head so
　　proud,
Have you not seen how pitiful lame he flies, and
　　none to befriend him?
Speak! Are you blind? Are you dead?
Shall we call him back? Shall we mend him?

BEING YOUNG AND GREEN

BEING young and green, I said in love's despite:
Never in the world will I to living wight
Give over, air my mind
To anyone,
Hang out its ancient secrets in the strong wind
To be shredded and faded. . . .

Oh, me, invaded
And sacked by the wind and the sun!

MIST IN THE VALLEY

THESE hills, to hurt me more,
That am hurt already enough,—
Having left the sea behind,
Having turned suddenly and left the shore
That I had loved beyond all words, even a song's
      words, to convey,

And built me a house on upland acres,
Sweet with the pinxter, bright and rough
With the rusty blackbird long before the winter's
      done,
But smelling never of bayberry hot in the sun,
Nor ever loud with the pounding of the long white
      breakers,—

These hills, beneath the October moon,
Sit in the valley white with mist
Like islands in a quiet bay,

Jut out from shore into the mist,
Wooded with poplar dark as pine,
Like points of land into a quiet bay.

(Just in that way
The harbour met the bay)

Stricken too sore for tears,
I stand, remembering the islands and the sea's lost
     sound. . . .
Life at its best no longer than the sand-peep's cry,
And I two years, two years,
Tilling an upland ground!

THE HARDY GARDEN

Now LET forever the phlox and the rose be tended
Here where the rain has darkened and the sun has
    dried
So many times the terrace, yet is love unended,
  Love has not died.

Let here no seed of a season, that the winter
But once assails, take root and for a time endure;
But only such as harbour at the frozen centre
  The germ secure.

Set here the phlox and the iris, and establish
Pink and valerian, and the great and lesser bells;
But suffer not the sisters of the year, to publish
  That frost prevails.

How far from home in a world of mortal burdens
Is Love, that may not die, and is forever young!
Set roses here: surround her only with such maidens
  As speak her tongue.

THE PIGEONS

Well I remember the pigeons in the sunny arbor
Beyond your open door;
How they conversed throughout the afternoon in
their monotonous voices never for a moment
still;
Always of yesterday they spoke, and of the days
before,
Rustling the vine-leaves, twitching the dark shadows of the leaves on the bright sill.

You said, the soft curring and droning of the
pigeons in the vine
Was a pretty thing enough to the passer-by,
But a maddening thing to the man with his head
in his hands,—"Like mine! Like mine!"
You said, and ran to the door and waved them off
into the sky.

They did not come back. The arbor was empty of
their cooing.
The shadows of the leaves were still. "Whither
have they flown, then?"
I said, and waited for their wings, but they did not
come back. If I had known then
What I know now, I never would have left your
door.

Tall in your faded smock, with steady hand
Mingling the brilliant pigments, painting your
    intersecting planes you stand,
In a quiet room, empty of the past, of its droning
    and cooing,
Thinking I know not what, but thinking of me no
    more,
That left you with a light word, that loving and
    rueing
Walk in the streets of a city you have never seen,
Walk in a noise of yesterday and of the days
    before,
Walk in a cloud of wings intolerable, shutting out
    the sun as if it never had been.

THE BUCK IN THE SNOW

White sky, over the hemlocks bowed with snow,
Saw you not at the beginning of evening the antlered
buck and his doe
Standing in the apple-orchard? I saw them. I saw
them suddenly go,
Tails up, with long leaps lovely and slow,
Over the stone-wall into the wood of hemlocks
bowed with snow.

Now lies he here, his wild blood scalding the snow.

How strange a thing is death, bringing to his knees,
bringing to his antlers
The buck in the snow.
How strange a thing,—a mile away by now, it may
be,
Under the heavy hemlocks that as the moments
pass
Shift their loads a little, letting fall a feather of
snow—
Life, looking out attentive from the eyes of the doe.

PART TWO

THE ANGUISH

I WOULD to God I were quenched and fed
As in my youth
From the flask of song, and the good bread
Of beauty richer than truth.

The anguish of the world is on my tongue.
My bowl is filled to the brim with it; there is more
      than I can eat.
Happy are the toothless old and the toothless
      young,
That cannot rend this meat.

JUSTICE DENIED IN MASSACHUSETTS

Let us abandon then our gardens and go home
And sit in the sitting-room.
Shall the larkspur blossom or the corn grow under
    this cloud?
Sour to the fruitful seed
Is the cold earth under this cloud,
Fostering quack and weed, we have marched upon
    but cannot conquer;
We have bent the blades of our hoes against the
    stalks of them.

Let us go home, and sit in the sitting-room.
Not in our day
Shall the cloud go over and the sun rise as before,
Beneficent upon us
Out of the glittering bay,
And the warm winds be blown inward from the sea
Moving the blades of corn
With a peaceful sound.
Forlorn, forlorn,
Stands the blue hay-rack by the empty mow.
And the petals drop to the ground,
Leaving the tree unfruited.
The sun that warmed our stooping backs and with-
    ered the weed uprooted—

We shall not feel it again.
We shall die in darkness, and be buried in the rain.

What from the splendid dead
We have inherited—
Furrows sweet to the grain, and the weed subdued—
See now the slug and the mildew plunder.
Evil does overwhelm
The larkspur and the corn;
We have seen them go under.

Let us sit here, sit still,
Here in the sitting-room until we die;
At the step of Death on the walk, rise and go;
Leaving to our children's children this beautiful
    doorway,
And this elm,
And a blighted earth to till
With a broken hoe.

Before the cock in the barnyard spoke,
  Before it well was day,
Horror like a serpent from about the Hangman's
    Oak
  Uncoiled and slid away.

Pity and Peace were on the limb
  That bore such bitter fruit.
Deep he lies, and the desperate blood of him
  Befriends the innocent root.

Brother, I said to the air beneath the bough
  Whence he had swung,
It will not be long for any of us now;
  We do not grow young.

It will not be long for the knotter of ropes, not long
  For the sheriff or for me,
Or for any of them that came five hundred strong
  To see you swing from a tree.

Side by side together in the belly of Death
  We sit without hope,
You, and I, and the mother that gave you breath,
  And the tree, and the rope.

WINE FROM THESE GRAPES

Wine from these grapes I shall be treading surely
Morning and noon and night until I die.
Stained with these grapes I shall lie down to die.

If you would speak with me on any matter,
At any time, come where these grapes are grown;
And you will find me treading them to must.
Lean then above me sagely, lest I spatter
Drops of the wine I tread from grapes and dust.

Stained with these grapes I shall lie down to die.
Three women come to wash me clean
Shall not erase this stain.
Nor leave me lying purely,
Awaiting the black lover.
Death, fumbling to uncover
My body in his bed,
Shall know
There has been one
Before him.

TO THOSE WITHOUT PITY

CRUEL of heart, lay down my song.
Your reading eyes have done me wrong.
Not for you was the pen bitten,
And the mind wrung, and the song written.

PART THREE

DAWN

ALL men are lonely now.
This is the hour when no man has a friend.
Memory and Faith suspend
From their spread wings above a cool abyss.
All friendships end.

He that lay awake
All night
For sweet love's unregenerate sake,
Sleeps in the grey light.

The lover, if he dream at all,
Dreams not of her whose languid hand sleeps open
    at his side;
He is gone to another bride.
And she he leaves behind
Sighs not in sleep "Unkind . . . unkind . . .";
She walks in a garden of yellow quinces;
Smiling, she gathers yellow quinces in a basket
Of willow and laurel combined.

Should I return to your door,
Fresh and haggard out of the morning air,
There would be darkness on the stair,
And a dead close odor painfully sad,

That was not there before.
There would be silence. There would be heavy
    steps across the floor.
And you would let me in, frowning with sleep
Under your rumpled hair.

Beautiful now upon the ear unshut by slumber
The rich and varied voices of the waking day!—
The mighty, mournful whistles without number
Of tugs and ferries, mingling, confounding, failing,
Thinning to separate notes of wailing,
Making stupendous music on the misty bay.

Now through the echoing street in the growing light,
Intent on errands that the sun approves,
Clatter unashamed the heavy wheels and hooves
Before the silent houses; briskly they say:
"Marshal not me among the enterprises of the
    night.
I am the beginning of the day."

TO A YOUNG GIRL

Shall I despise you that your colourless tears
Made rainbows in your lashes, and you forgot to
    weep?
Would we were half so wise, that eke a grief out
By sitting in the dark, until we fall asleep.

I only fear lest, being by nature sunny,
By and by you will weep no more at all,
And fall asleep in the light, having lost with the
    tears
The colour in the lashes that comes as the tears fall.

I would not have you darken your lids with weep-
    ing,
Beautiful eyes, but I would have you weep enough
To wet the fingers of the hand held over the eye-lids,
And stain a little the light frock's delicate stuff.

For there came into my mind, as I watched you
    winking the tears down,
Laughing faces, blown from the west and the east,
Faces lovely and proud that I have prized and
    cherished;
Nor were the loveliest among them those that had
    wept the least.

EVENING ON LESBOS

Twice having seen your shingled heads adorable
Side by side, the onyx and the gold,
I know that I have had what I could not hold.

Twice have I entered the room, not knowing she
    was here.
Two agate eyes, two eyes of malachite,
Twice have been turned upon me, hard and bright.

Whereby I know my loss.
                        Oh, not restorable
Sweet incense, mounting in the windless night!

DIRGE WITHOUT MUSIC

I AM not resigned to the shutting away of loving
    hearts in the hard ground.
So it is, and so it will be, for so it has been, time
    out of mind:
Into the darkness they go, the wise and the lovely.
    Crowned
With lilies and with laurel they go; but I am not
    resigned.

Lovers and thinkers, into the earth with you.
Be one with the dull, the indiscriminate dust.
A fragment of what you felt, of what you knew,
A formula, a phrase remains,—but the best is lost.

The answers quick and keen, the honest look, the
    laughter, the love,—
They are gone. They are gone to feed the roses.
    Elegant and curled
Is the blossom. Fragrant is the blossom. I know.
    But I do not approve.
More precious was the light in your eyes than all
    the roses of the world.

Down, down, down into the darkness of the grave
Gently they go, the beautiful, the tender, the kind;
Quietly they go, the intelligent, the witty, the brave.
I know. But I do not approve. And I am not
  resigned.

MEMORY OF CASSIS

Do you recall how we sat by the smokily-burning
Twisted odorous trunk of the olive-tree,
In the inn on the cliff, and skinned the ripe green
     figs,
And heard the white sirocco driving in the sea?

The thunder and the smother there where like a
     ship's prow
The light-house breasted the wave? how wanly
     through the wild spray
Under our peering eyes the eye of the light looked
     out,
Disheveled, but without dismay?

Do you recall the sweet-alyssum over the ledges
Crawling and the tall heather and the mushrooms
     under the pines,
And the deep white dust of the broad road leading
     outward
To a world forgotten, between the dusty almonds
     and the dusty vines?

PORTRAIT

Over and over I have heard,
As now I hear it,
Your voice harsh and light as the scratching of dry
leaves over the hard ground,
Your voice forever assailed and shaken by the wind
from the island
Of illustrious living and dead, that never dies down,
And bending at moments under the terrible weight
of the perfect word,
Here in this room without fire, without comfort of
any kind,
Reading aloud to me immortal page after page con-
ceived in a mortal mind.
Beauty at such moments before me like a wild
bright bird
Has been in the room, and eyed me, and let me
come near it.

I could not ever nor can I to this day
Acquaint you with the triumph and the sweet rest
These hours have brought to me and always bring,—
Rapture, coloured like the wild bird's neck and
wing,
Comfort, softer than the feathers of its breast.

Always, and even now, when I rise to go,
Your eyes blaze out from a face gone wickedly pale;
I try to tell you what I would have you know,—
What peace it was; you cry me down; you scourge
    me with a salty flail;
You will not have it so.

WINTER NIGHT

PILE high the hickory and the light
Log of chestnut struck by the blight.
Welcome-in the winter night.

The day has gone in hewing and felling,
Sawing and drawing wood to the dwelling
For the night of talk and story-telling.

These are the hours that give the edge
To the blunted axe and the bent wedge,
Straighten the saw and lighten the sledge.

Here are question and reply,
And the fire reflected in the thinking eye.
So peace, and let the bob-cat cry.

THE CAMEO

FOREVER over now, forever, forever gone
That day. Clear and diminished like a scene
Carven in cameo, the lighthouse, and the cove
    between
The sandy cliffs, and the boat drawn up on the
    beach;
And the long skirt of a lady innocent and young,
Her hand resting on her bosom, her head hung;
And the figure of a man in earnest speech.

Clear and diminished like a scene cut in cameo
The lighthouse, and the boat on the beach, and
    the two shapes
Of the woman and the man; lost like the lost day
Are the words that passed, and the pain,—dis-
    carded, cut away
From the stone, as from the memory the heat of
    the tears escapes.

O troubled forms, O early love unfortunate and
    hard,
Time has estranged you into a jewel cold and pure;
From the action of the waves and from the action
    of sorrow forever secure,
White against a ruddy cliff you stand, chalcedony
    on sard.

COUNTING-OUT RHYME

Silver bark of beech, and sallow
Bark of yellow birch and yellow
   Twig of willow.

Stripe of green in moosewood maple,
Colour seen in leaf of apple,
   Bark of popple.

Wood of popple pale as moonbeam,
Wood of oak for yoke and barn-beam,
   Wood of hornbeam.

Silver bark of beech, and hollow
Stem of elder, tall and yellow
   Twig of willow.

THE PLUM GATHERER

The angry nettle and the mild
  Grew together under the blue-plum trees.
I could not tell as a child
  Which was my friend of these.

Always the angry nettle in the skirt of his sister
  Caught my wrist that reached over the ground,
Where alike I gathered,—for the one was sweet
    and the other wore a frosty dust—
  The broken plum and the sound.

The plum-trees are barren now and the black knot
    is upon them,
  That stood so white in the spring.
I would give, to recall the sweetness and the frost
    of the lost blue plums,
  Anything, anything.
I thrust my arm among the grey ambiguous nettles,
    and wait.
  But they do not sting.

WEST COUNTRY SONG

Sun came up, bigger than all my sorrow;
Lark in air so high, and his song clean through me.
Now comes night, hushing the lark in's furrow,
And the rain falls fine.
What have I done with what was dearest to me?

Thatch and wick, fagot, and tea on trivet,—
These and more it was; it was all my cheer.
Now comes night, smelling of box and privet,
    And the rain falls fine.
Have I left it out in the rain?—It is not here.

PUEBLO POT

There as I bent above the broken pot from the
    mesa pueblo,
Mournfully many times its patterned shards piecing
    together and laying aside,
Appeared upon the house-top, two Navajos en-
    chanted, the red-shafted flicker and his bride,
And stepped with lovely stride
To the pergola, flashing the wonder of their under-
    wings;
There stood, mysterious and harsh and sleek,
Wrenching the indigo berry from the shedding
    woodbine with strong ebony beak.

His head without a crest
Wore the red full moon for crown;
The black new moon was crescent on the breast
Of each;
From the bodies of both a visible heat beat down,
And from the motion of their necks a shadow
    would fly and fall,
Skimming the court and in the yellow adobe wall
Cleaving a blue breach.

Powerful was the beauty of these birds.
It boomed like a struck bell in the silence deep
    and hot.

I stooped above the shattered clay; passionately I
    cried to the beauty of these birds,
"Solace the broken pot!"

The beauty of these birds
Opened its lips to speak;
Colours were its words,
The scarlet shaft on the grey cheek,
The purple berry in the ebony beak.
It said, "I cannot console
The broken thing; I can only make it whole."

Wisdom, heretic flower, I was ever afraid
Of your large, cool petals without scent!
Shocked, betrayed,
I turned to the comfort of grief, I bent
Above the lovely shards.
But their colours had faded in the fierce light of
    the birds.
And as for the birds, they were gone. As suddenly
    as they had come, they went.

WHEN CAESAR FELL

When Caesar fell, where yellow Tiber rolls
   Its heavy waters muddy,
Life, that was ebbing from a hundred holes
   In Caesar's body,
Cried with a hundred voices to the common air,
   The unimperial day,
"Gather me up, oh, pour me into the veins of even
     a gilder of hair!
   Let me not vanish away!"

The teeth of Caesar at the ignoble word
   Were ground together in pride;
No sound came from his lips: the world has heard
   How Caesar died.
In the Roman dust the cry of Caesar's blood
   Was heard and heard without wonder
Only by the fly that swam in the red flood
   Till his head went under.

LETHE

Ah, drink again
This river that is the taker-away of pain,
And the giver-back of beauty!

In these cool waves
What can be lost?—
Only the sorry cost
Of the lovely thing, ah, never the thing itself!

The level flood that laves
The hot brow
And the stiff shoulder
Is at our temples now.

Gone is the fever,
But not into the river;
Melted the frozen pride,
But the tranquil tide
Runs never the warmer for this,
Never the colder.

Immerse the dream.
Drench the kiss.
Dip the song in the stream.

ON FIRST HAVING HEARD
THE SKYLARK

NOT knowing he rose from earth, not having seen
    him rise,
Not knowing the fallow furrow was his home,
And that high wing, untouchable, untainted,
A wing of earth, with the warm loam
Closely acquainted,
I shuddered at his cry and caught my heart.
Relentless out of heaven his sweet crying like a
    crystal dart
Was launched against me. Scanning the empty sky
I stood with thrown-back head until the world
    reeled.
Still, still he sped his unappeasable shafts against
    my breast without a shield.
He cried forever from his unseen throat
Between me and the sun.
He would not end his singing, he would not have
    done.
"Serene and pitiless note, whence, whence are you?"
I cried. "Alas, these arrows, how fast they fall!
Ay, me, beset by angels in unequal fight,
Alone high on the shaven down surprised, and not
    a tree in sight!"

Even as I spoke he was revealed
Above me in the bright air,
A dark articulate atom in the mute enormous
blue,
A mortal bird, flying and singing in the morning
there.
Even as I spoke I spied him, and I knew,
And called him by his name;
"Blithe Spirit!" I cried. Transfixed by more than
mortal spears
I fell; I lay among the foreign daisies pink and
small,
And wept, staining their innocent faces with fast-
flowing tears.

TO A MUSICIAN

WHO, now, when evening darkens the water and
    the stream is dull,
Slowly, in a delicate frock, with her leghorn hat in
    her hand,
At your side from under the golden osiers moves,
Faintly smiling, shattered by the charm of your
    voice?

There, today, as in the days when I knew you well,
The willow sheds upon the stream its narrow leaves,
And the quiet flowing of the water and its faint smell
Are balm to the heart that grieves.

Together with the sharp discomfort of loving you,
Ineffable you, so lovely and so aloof,
There is laid upon the spirit the calmness of the
    river view:
Together they fall, the pain and its reproof.

Who, now, under the yellow willows at the water's
    edge
Closes defeated lips upon the trivial word unspoken,
And lifts her soft eyes freighted with a heavy pledge
To your eyes empty of pledges, even of pledges
    broken?

PART FOUR

SONNET

Life, were thy pains as are the pains of hell,
So hardly to be borne, yet to be borne,
And all thy boughs more grim with wasp and thorn
Than armoured bough stood ever; too chill to spell
With the warm tongue, and sharp with broken
    shell
Thy ways, whereby in wincing haste forlorn
The desperate foot must travel, blind and torn,
Yet must I cry,—So be it; it is well.

So fair to me thy vineyards, nor less fair
Than the sweet heaven my fathers hoped to gain;
So bright this earthly blossom spiked with care,
This harvest hung behind the boughs of pain,
Needs must I gather, guessing by the stain
I bleed, but know not wherefore, know not where.

SONNET

GROW not too high, grow not too far from home,
Green tree, whose roots are in the granite's face!
Taller than silver spire or golden dome
A tree may grow above its earthy place,
And taller than a cloud, but not so tall
The root may not be mother to the stem,
Lifting rich plenty, though the rivers fall,
To the cold sunny leaves to nourish them.
Have done with blossoms for a time, be bare;
Split rock; plunge downward; take heroic soil;
Deeper than bones—no pasture for you there;
Deeper than water, deeper than gold and oil:
Earth's fiery core alone can feed the bough
That blooms between Orion and the Plough.

SONNET TO GATH

COUNTRY of hunchbacks!— where the strong,
    straight spine,
Jeered at by crooked children, makes his way
Through by-streets at the kindest hour of day,
Till he deplore his stature, and incline
To measure manhood with a gibbous line;
Till out of loneliness, being flawed with clay,
He stoop into his neighbour's house and say,
"Your roof is low for me—the fault is mine."

Dust in an urn long since, dispersed and dead
Is great Apollo; and the happier he;
Since who amongst you all would lift a head
At a god's radiance on the mean door-tree,
Saving to run and hide your dates and bread,
And cluck your children in about your knee?

THE PIONEER

On the Unveiling of a Statue to Lucretia Mott, Susan B. Anthony, and Elizabeth Cady Stanton. Washington, November eighteenth, 1923.

Upon this marble bust that is not I
Lay the round, formal wreath that is not fame;
But in the forum of my silenced cry
Root ye the living tree whose sap is flame.
I, that was proud and valiant, am no more;—
Save as a dream that wanders wide and late,
Save as a wind that rattles the stout door,
Troubling the ashes in the sheltered grate.
The stone will perish; I shall be twice dust.
Only my standard on a taken hill
Can cheat the mildew and the red-brown rust
And make immortal my adventurous will.
　　Even now the silk is tugging at the staff:
　　Take up the song; forget the epitaph.

TO JESUS ON HIS BIRTHDAY

For this your mother sweated in the cold,
For this you bled upon the bitter tree:
A yard of tinsel ribbon bought and sold;
A paper wreath; a day at home for me.
The merry bells ring out, the people kneel;
Up goes the man of God before the crowd;
With voice of honey and with eyes of steel
He drones your humble gospel to the proud.
Nobody listens. Less than the wind that blows
Are all your words to us you died to save.
O Prince of Peace! O Sharon's dewy Rose!
How mute you lie within your vaulted grave.
   The stone the angel rolled away with tears
   Is back upon your mouth these thousand years.

SONNET

NOT that it matters, not that my heart's cry
Is potent to deflect our common doom,
Or bind to truce in this ambiguous room
The planets of the atom as they ply;
But only to record that you and I,
Like thieves that scratch the jewels from a tomb,
Have gathered delicate love in hardy bloom
Close under Chaos,—I rise to testify.
This is my testament: that we are taken;
Our colours are as clouds before the wind;
Yet for a moment stood the foe forsaken,
Eyeing Love's favour to our helmet pinned;
Death is our master,—but his seat is shaken;
He rides victorious,—but his ranks are thinned.

ON HEARING A SYMPHONY OF
BEETHOVEN

SWEET sounds, oh, beautiful music, do not cease!
Reject me not into the world again.
With you alone is excellence and peace,
Mankind made plausible, his purpose plain.
Enchanted in your air benign and shrewd,
With limbs a-sprawl and empty faces pale,
The spiteful and the stingy and the rude
Sleep like the scullions in the fairy-tale.
This moment is the best the world can give:
The tranquil blossom on the tortured stem.
Reject me not, sweet sounds! oh, let me live,
Till Doom espy my towers and scatter them,
A city spell-bound under the aging sun,
Music my rampart, and my only one.

THE HOUSE OF HARPER

NEW YORK

Publishers of BOOKS and of

HARPER'S MAGAZINE

Established 1817